If the
CR⬡WN
Fits...

28 Doable Devos to
Discover You're Royalty

Loveland, CO

Group
Real. **Bold**. Love.

If the Crown Fits...

28 Doable Devos to Discover You're Royalty

Visit our websites:

group.com
group.com/women

Unless otherwise indicated, all Scripture quotations are taken from the *Holy Bible*, New Living Translation, copyright © 1996, 2004, 2007 by Tyndale House Foundation. Used by permission of Tyndale House Publishers, Inc., Carol Stream, Illinois 60188. All rights reserved.

ISBN 978-1-4707-1368-3

Printed in the United States of America.

10 9 8 7 6 5 4 3 2 1   23 22 21 20 19 18 17 16 15 14

Dedicated to Melissa, who has always helped me find my crown.

The world is coming to an end. The swift air of agony drifts past as the mountains fall and volcanoes erupt. Even the sea creatures are finding refuge to protect themselves from Armageddon. All of this in response to the inability to fit into the little black dress, make an additional $10,000, and have a handsome, successful husband to parade around at the next event. Simply put, this princess would rather see the earth crumble than attend the ball and explain why she's just a maid in the castle.

My dear friend Melissa has been privy to my slightly exaggerated lack of confidence like this on several occasions. Time after time I have been off in my own little world until a crisis hits. One month till some giant event that I am not nearly proud enough of myself to attend. Other times it was just a need to feel good about myself after a breakup or a hard time in life. Wait! Shouldn't we feel good about ourselves every day?

Her advice: Buy some earrings. I laughed, bought some earrings, and felt better. Amazingly, shifting my focus from the gaping chasm of my unworthiness to a little bit of something sparkly made my mood sparkle too. No, this is not a book about freedom to spend for shopaholics. In fact, I was planning on writing a book that simply poked fun at self-help books by encouraging all sorts of frivolous things to improve self-esteem. However, being the lifelong learner that I am, I started researching. (You do have to know what is going on in the world to make fun of it

properly.) Much to my surprise, I hit a little road bump in my research. The "frivolous" things my girlfriends and I encouraged each other to do to help improve our moods are scientifically proven ways to discourage depression.

Now we are onto something.

Unfortunately, like many women we need to be told to do something good for ourselves. We need to know it's okay. We need to believe that somehow we are allowed to feel special. Guess what? We are, and we do deserve it. We deserve to be princesses every day. But being a princess is much more than buying earrings and new dresses when you are feeling down. That would be a lifestyle tempting a budgetary deficit that rivals government spending. No. Being a princess is much more complex than that.

Although the Disney princesses typically fall in love with Prince Charming in one day at age 16, it's still pretty clear they are loved for more than their youth and beauty. They are kind, generous, appreciative...happy. This is your opportunity to invite joy into your life on a daily basis for 28 days.

What will you be doing for the next 28 days? Every princess knows there is only one motivational tool that will keep you focused. You must keep your eye on the C.R.O.W.N. However, you're not aspiring to win the swimsuit competition with double-stick tape stuck to your tush or the evening gown event via Vaseline on your teeth for a stick-proof smile. No, your goal is to feel like a princess. To feel like you have the world at your fingertips. Therefore, your crown may not be 12 inches tall and studded with diamonds. Your crown is actually much taller and perhaps even more challenging to attain. Your crown fills up your life with a new appreciation for the God who gave you your princess heart, the relationships he has placed in your life, the beauty in the world around you, and YOU—just as you are, daughter of the King...a princess.

Keep Your Eye on the C.R.O.W.N.

Each day as we work on revealing our princess selves, we'll be focusing on our C.R.O.W.N.

Credo

Bible verses to live by. Jesus Christ inspires, motivates, encourages, comforts, and loves all his daughters.

Respect

Respect encompasses you, others, God, and his creation. Learning to take the time to appreciate everyone and everything around you is definitely a royal quality.

Ornamentation

Yes. This is the part where we get to buy earrings and new clothes. However, there will be a few surprises along the way. Don't underestimate where you can find beauty.

Workout

Working out is about fitness, not your figure. There are definitely physical benefits of being active for your body, but working out makes you feel better.

Nutrition

Have you ever heard the saying "You are what you eat?" Guess what. You are. What you eat is the only thing your body has to work with to make new cells and keep your body moving. Paying attention to this little part of life will make a huge difference in how you feel physically and emotionally.

Credo

Anyone who has grown up in the church has probably been asked to memorize Bible verses at some point in time, while those outside the church might consider the Good Book to be a little overwhelming and too mysterious to want to dig into. So why is it important to start the princess journey in its pages? Because it is your connection to your King.

Sleeping Beauty had a curse placed on her at her birthday bash and was whisked away to the forest to protect her from death. She grew up without the knowledge of her royal status, but she was still kind-hearted and generous because she was literally living in a fairy tale. Back in the real world many women seem to be living in a fairy tale, but, sadly, more often than not these fairy tale facades are just that—smiley faces painted on the outside of empty hearts waiting for a reason to feel more.

Cut to the kingdom. Mom and dad, the king and queen, are anxiously awaiting the arrival of their pretty princess so they can unite her with the prince and watch her live happily ever after. Instead of thinking her parents could have any idea who would bring her happiness, she decides some prince is being imposed on her and keeping her from the happiness she seeks with a stranger in the woods. Little does she know this is exactly who her parents have planned for her. The king has put in place guidelines for a life she has yet to imagine.

How is this applicable to you? You have *the* King in your corner, the end-all be-all, the King of kings, making you the princess of princesses because you are God's child. How can you make yourself believe it? To steal some words from Dr. Phil, "Fake it till you make it"— daily affirmations repeated until you actually believe what you're telling yourself. Of course, this means you can't just mutter "I'm a princess" under your breath and expect to order your ball gown and book your magical carriage tomorrow. You need to say it like you mean it. Look in the mirror and repeat to yourself several times the credo of the day. Make a sticky note of your favorites and put it on your mirror, in your car, at your desk...anywhere that you will be continually reminded of the important wisdom that is freely yours to apply to your life.

But how? This is where the Bible takes center stage. God doesn't tell lies, and he has a book full of promises and love expressing just how special you are. A book full of guidelines outlining how you attain your fairy tale ending. It may be easier to believe in a pumpkin turning into a carriage at first, but eventually you'll know that God thinks you're wonderful. And, of course, you're not going to think God is wrong. Remember, how God made you is amazing and wonderful.

If the CROWN Fits...

Respect

Aretha Franklin is considered the queen of R&B, and she knew what she was talking about when she sang about R.E.S.P.E.C.T. Respect plays a huge role in how one approaches any person or occasion. Imagine, for instance, how you'd react when the prom king asks you to dance versus when, at the same prom, your biochem partner, who hasn't yet discovered the need for deodorant, asks for the last dance. Who would you choose? (Be honest!)

Now take the same two people, and in your biochem class your teacher says the final exam may be taken with a partner and your final grade is determined by the outcome of this test. It's obvious you would spray on some extra perfume and race to the smartest person in class while smelling the sweet scent of an acceptance letter from Harvard.

You see, while you appreciate and respect the beauty and charm of the prom king at the dance, you know that his looks won't help you get into college. Every person and every situation has the appropriate time or specialty to be respected. You just need to take the time to recognize what it is.

The best way to start feeling respected and appreciated is to start respecting and appreciating others. When the focus shifts from you to those around you, you become a magnetic force attracting kindness and love. Of course, you don't live in far, far away—you live in the real world where people are going to mess up and forget your princess status and the respect and appreciation that comes with the crown. They may hurt your feelings. You may also unintentionally hurt their feelings. However, you are a princess. You will learn the value of yourself and others in your life. After all, God made you...but he also made them. Better to share the love than to start princess-pouting until the whole kingdom is in a tizzy. Because we all know if the princess ain't happy...ain't nobody happy. Or is that just how it seems?

When a princess is never without her mirror—ensuring she is the most tan, whitened-teeth, smooth-skinned of them all—she may actually be letting down the kingdom. On the other hand, if you're the princess stuck in a tower turning into an ogre at night, there are very few people who are going to be too concerned about doing anything to help you keep your crown on straight during the daylight hours. Think for a moment...

Why would anyone feel you are worthy of respect if you don't respect yourself?

Why would anyone want to respect you if you, in turn, do not respect anyone around you?

Ornamentation

After a day of dismal drippings of gloom, my mother noticed her princess was not as perky as normal and suggested a pair of earrings. "You'll look so much happier," she said. Of course, I responded as any princess would by thanking my mother dearest for her concern and instantly perking up, living happily ever after. Okay, the truth is this scene more closely resembled a 14-year-old's temper tantrum, which is unfortunate, especially since I was in my mid-20s at the time. We still joke about how much happier I look when wearing earrings.

The funny thing is, it's true. When you feel pretty, you feel happier. The secret is *allowing* yourself to feel pretty. In a world gone wrong, you're inundated with images telling you that you're not good enough. Not pretty enough. Not young enough. Not rich enough. Yet you are exactly as God created you, and he doesn't make junk. It's your job to appreciate this amazing self God gave you. No longer will you get a compliment and brush it off or try to minimize it because you don't believe it. You will say thank you. If you're not quite to the point of believing it yourself, just accept that someone else thinks you're wonderful. Eventually you'll catch on that they're right.

Ornamentation does not always come in the form of new clothes, makeup, or even earrings. At times you will take *away* ornamentation to see the beauty, or you'll focus on seeing it in other people, your surroundings, or yourself. During the next 28 days you'll take some time to slow down and see all the beauty that God has placed in your life. I'm pretty sure it wasn't an accident when he finished each day of creation with "It is good," and I'm guessing that is the minimum God thought when he created you.

Another great way to feel prettier (and thus happier) is to surround yourself with beauty. Sometimes you just need to clean up something to make it beautiful or add a little sparkle. Other times you simply need to take the time to notice there is more going on in the world than the wrinkle across your forehead or pimple jumping off your face with a neon sign saying, "Look at me!" Instead, look below that pimple...a little lower...lower... yes, right there at that gorgeous smile. Look at how your grandmother's eyes still sparkle when she talks about meeting dear old gramps. See the dandelion poking through the crack in the sidewalk. The squirrels flirting their way up a tree. The joy on the face of a child who watercolored a masterpiece just for you. I could go on forever.

There is beauty. Everywhere.

Workout

You have to spend energy to make energy, and a princess definitely has energy. There is no need for a princess to complete an Ironman Triathlon, but you can always try. Similarly, there is no reason to complete a total body transformation. You still want to be recognized when you've completed the princess process. Instead, let's focus on something simple. Feeling better. Having enough energy to act like a princess and enough happiness to share with your little kingdom.

When exercise happens in the body a special little hormone called endorphins are released, which really do improve your mood. Maybe there is something behind that crazy dance aerobics instructor's perky smile matching her other perky parts. Feeling good and looking good go hand in hand like peanut butter and jelly, cookies and milk, burritos and guacamole. (Miss Perky in spandex is probably not partaking in too many of those, but we will get to that later.)

The exercises we spotlight each day may seem easy or difficult or not like exercise at all. That's because everything you do affects your body. What you're doing with your body translates to what parts of your body are strong, how you carry yourself, and, yes, what dress size you wear. However, most princesses have their dresses custom made so there is no need to worry about what size you are. Instead, the focus is on how you are feeling and if it makes you act like a princess.

The basic elements of a healthy exercise plan involve cardiovascular training, strength building, and flexibility.

Cardiovascular training is probably what comes to mind when someone thinks of "having to exercise" — running for miles on end or getting confused in some exercise dance class. It can be agonizing, or it can also be fun. The primary goal of cardiovascular exercise is to strengthen your heart. It kind of has a big job, so it's good to take care of it. One does this by increasing the heart rate and keeping it at that increased level for a sustained period of time. Walking, dancing, playing on the playground, and chasing down Prince Charming are all fun ways to include activity in your day.

Strength building or resistance training is what will help build your muscle mass. Don't worry, you won't end up looking like a female Arnold Schwarzenegger; you simply don't have enough testosterone to get crazy. Instead, this will help you be able to do more princess duties and burn more calories even when you're resting. What a royal idea!

Flexibility is the fancy version of stretching, lengthening the muscle tissue. After all that weight lifting, you'll need to stretch it back out. Plus proper stretching helps one avoid injury and may improve performance.

*Please be advised these are general exercise suggestions, and if you have any questions about your ability and/or safety in completing the task at hand, consult your doctor.

Nutrition

You are what you eat. Everyone has heard this familiar phrase at one point or another. On the days you're filling yourself with a delectable combination of fast food, diet sodas, and meal replacement bars you're probably feeling a little sluggish compared to days when you get to sit down to a good, old-fashioned meal. You know, the kind with meat and vegetables...at a table. Think about it this way, if you were making a skyscraper and you were fortunate enough to have dibs on the penthouse, would you want to build it out of carrots or french fries? (I understand it's unlikely that these are the only building materials available, but this *is* a book about princesses and fairy tales and make believe.) I'm guessing you'd choose carrots, a firm building material that the big bad wolf himself has very little interest in. (It's a good thing bacon wasn't an option.)

Why is your body, the temple of God, any different? If you want to make it feel firm and strong, you can't feed it ice cream and burritos. Trust me, I tried this diet for about six months and ended up stuffed like a sausage. (Not a very princess-like feeling.)

Even beyond how it makes you feel, what you eat is literally shaping your body. As princesses, I'm sure we can understand the value of the science, but I will put it in fairy-tale terms. When you eat something that is bad for you, it often contains horrible stepsisters called free radicals, destroying this beautiful body that was all dolled up for the ball and ripping it to shreds, leaving you in tears in the garden. Then your fairy godmother (antioxidants in good food) comes in to save the day, whipping up a sparkling dress, perfect hair with golden highlights, and even glass slippers—since they are the ideal choice for dancing all night, after all. The antioxidants basically hold the hand of the free radical, slowing them down so they can no longer do damage to your body, and you can arrive at the ball just in time for a quick dance before the clock strikes midnight. This means you show signs of aging more slowly and have more energy—the perfect image of a princess.

How does one transition from stepsister snacking to a diet even Cinderella would envy? Take baby steps and plan ahead. We will slowly discover ways to add foods into your day that will make you sparkle, getting others to take notice. After all, you can't eat dog food and expect to feel like a butterfly.

*If you have any specific dietary needs, please consult a doctor before making any changes to your diet.

C—Loved

"Watch what God does, and then you do it, like children who learn proper behavior from their parents. Mostly what God does is love you. Keep company with him and learn a life of love. Observe how Christ loved us. His love was not cautious but extravagant. He didn't love in order to get something from us but to give everything of himself to us. Love like that" (Ephesians 5:1-2, The Message).

God loves you just because you are. It might be hard to believe, but anything you do can't make him love you more. He sent his Son to die just for you. What more do you need to believe how much he loves you?

R—Feel the Love

Take a moment to sit back and really recognize God's extravagant love for you. Remember, love doesn't always look mushy-mushy. Sometimes love looks like protection, even when we don't want it. Think about how God might be loving you in areas that seem like a challenge or struggle right now. Remember, God knows the whole movie, not just this scene you're in right now.

O—Theme Song

Your life is far from insignificant. It's more like a blockbuster movie. Thus, the theme music is one of the most identifying features. It's your soundtrack. Pick a song that encapsulates who you are and who you want to continue becoming. It's great to have this on standby for those times that seem challenging, to help give you the strength to keep on keepin' on.

My Song: "You Say" by Lauren Daigle

W—Get Movin'

The easiest way to start adding energy to your day and sparkle to your attitude is to just move. We are going to start slow, so if you're already doing more just add these simple moves to your routine.

Start by parking as far away from your destination as possible. If you really have to get your Grande mocha with extra whip, then at least walk a little extra to get there.

N—Food Diary

The goal here is to gain health, not to become crazy calorie-counting carnivores. The best way to see your starting place is to start taking notes. Write down everything you eat today, the time you ate it, and how much you enjoyed it. It's amazing what you'll learn.

Time	Food	Did I enjoy it?
9:45	Toffeebar & Tea	Yes! Yumm

I'm ready! I can say I'm a daughter of a king but its been a long time since I've felt like one. I'm finding my priorities are different now and organizing my life, my habits are going to look different in 2019! I know life can get busy so help me to stay focused on whats important. I know life can get challenging so help me to keep my eyes on you! AMEN

C—A Princess

"So you are no longer a slave, but God's child; and since you are his child, God has made you also an heir" (Galatians 4:7, NIV).

Did you hear that? God just said you're his heir—which means you really are a princess, a daughter of the King.

R—Your Word

Take a moment just to think about who you are in the world and the gifts you contribute. Go into the bathroom. Shut the door and lock it. Look in the mirror. Look deep into who you are, who God made you to be. Now write down one word to describe you. Don't write a role that you fill but the essence of you.

Write that word here:

O—Five Extra Minutes

We'll start out easy and obvious. Take five extra minutes to make yourself feel pretty. We all know you already are, so why not take five extra minutes to appreciate 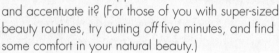 and accentuate it? (For those of you with super-sized beauty routines, try cutting *off* five minutes, and find some comfort in your natural beauty.)

W—Stand Tall

This may not seem like a "workout" but it is tremendously important for your health and confidence. God made you a princess—now stand tall and proud. Your posture communicates to the world what you think about yourself and how you should be treated. Your body should make a straight line through your ankle, knee, hip, shoulder, and ear. Stand tall for you and Jesus!

N—Food Diary

Yes, another day of writing down everything you eat. We need to make sure yesterday wasn't a feast or famine, just a normal day.

Time	Food	Did I enjoy it?
9	Bar w/ London FoG S.F.	YES
12	Kielbasa, protien Chips	

Thoughts from *Day 2*

_____

_____

_____

_____

_____

_____

_____

_____

_____

_____

_____

_____

_____

_____

_____

_____

_____

C – Complexity

"Thank you for making me so wonderfully complex!
Your workmanship is marvelous—how well I know it"
(Psalm 139:14).

Ponder that verse. The New International Reader's
Version simplifies it even more: "How you made me is
amazing and wonderful. I praise you for that." Surely a
princess believes such a bold statement, and you should
as well. Continue saying this verse until you believe it.
God does, so why shouldn't you?

R – What You Love

What is the last thing you did that you really loved? The kind
of thing that gave you more energy once you completed it
than when you began. Something you can't help but smile
about when you think of it. Remember, this is *something you
did*, not something that was done for you. A princess must
be able to create moments of pleasure and joy on her own.

O – Wear Jewelry

Don't go out and buy something new, just pick out
something you haven't worn in a while and go for it!

Even young girls know there is some special, warm, fuzzy feeling that grabs you like a bear hug from your Aunt Patty when you take the time to add a little sparkle. (If you're the type that feels naked without your adornments... minimize. The jewels you adorn yourself with cannot compete with the beauty that is you, so why try?)

W — Stretch It Out

We should all be shooting for 15 to 20 minutes a day of stretching, but princess schedules can be demanding so let's start small. Only two stretches today.

1. Stand with your feet together, legs straight, and let your body slowly bend over and hang, reaching as far to the ground as you can. You should feel this in the back of your legs and maybe into your lower back. Don't get uptight if you can't reach the floor; you're trying to stretch out those tight muscles.

2. Slowly stand upright, reach behind your back, grasp your hands together, and pull away from your body. You should feel your chest stretching out.

You will make progress as you continue including these simple stretches in your daily routine.

N—Food Diary

Will this ever end??? Yes. Today is day three and your final day of your food diary. You will be appreciative when it gets easier to see what improvements to make to your diet.

Time	Food	Did I enjoy it?

Thoughts from Day 3

_____

_____

_____

_____

_____

_____

_____

_____

_____

_____

_____

_____

DAY 4

C—Clothed With Beauty

"Don't be concerned about the outward beauty of fancy hairstyles, expensive jewelry, or beautiful clothes. You should clothe yourselves instead with the beauty that comes from within, the unfading beauty of a gentle and quiet spirit, which is so precious to God" (1 Peter 3:3-4).

If you are anything like me, a gentle and quiet spirit seems about as far away from where I am as possible. Honestly, I somewhat took offense to that portion of the verse. God made me loud. Shouldn't I embrace it? However, upon closer examination I realized this has a lot more to do with what's making me loud. Am I looking to gain attention for me or for the Lord?

R—Top Five Strengths

A wonderfully complex princess has a tremendous amount of strengths, so please try to limit yourself to your top five traits, talents, and abilities that God has given you to make you so special.

1.

2.

3.

4.

5.

O—Clean Your Space

Cleanliness is next to godliness, and the daughter of a King can't be living in a pigsty. Pick the space you spend the most time in and make it sparkle. It truly is good for the soul to spruce up your surroundings, boosting your energy and your feeling of accomplishment. Up next...Mount Everest?

W—Core Strength

This is a nice way to say work on those abs. Perhaps *your* motivation for continuous crunches is to have a bikini body in two weeks, but for the rest of us one-piecers, core strength is key to proper posture and reducing back injury. Strengthening your abs doesn't take long—you can do it at your desk. Suck in your belly button to your spine and hold it there for 10 to 15 seconds. Release, and do it again. You can do this all day long. Just make sure you're holding your abs and not your breath.

N—Food Diary Review

Observe your notes from the past three days. Look for healthy choices you are already making in addition to possible improvements. Moderation is key. Look for a healthy distribution of wholesome nutrition. Whole grains, dairy, fruits, veggies, and lean meats. If you have special dietary needs or are vegetarian, be sure you have consulted a professional to make sure you are getting enough of the proper nutrients for your body.

Thoughts from *Day 4*

_____

_____

_____

_____

_____

_____

_____

_____

_____

_____

_____

_____

_____

C—Radiant

"I prayed to the Lord, and he answered me. He freed me from all my fears. Those who look to him for help will be radiant with joy; no shadow of shame will darken their faces" (Psalm 34:4-5).

There is no need to fear when you look to God. Wouldn't you rather be radiant instead of living in a shadow?

R—Five Weaknesses

This isn't a typo. Even princesses have weaknesses, and let's face it, weaknesses are scary. We lose power, control, order, and comfort. Now you have two choices: do something about it or release it. Write your list of five weaknesses, and then carefully go through it and make a plan for improvement. Or give it to God. On a piece of paper, write down the things you are giving to God, and then rip up the paper. It's gone now; you don't need it.

1.

2.

3.

4.

5.

O—Dress Up

A princess is not about to dwell on the weaknesses she has to work through. She has recognized where growth can happen, made a plan, and is working to become an even better princess. Now it's time for the princess to work her princess self. Pick out something you haven't worn in a while and make it shout out how amazing you are—even if it's just around the house.

W—Upper Body Strength

The strength of a princess can be seen in many admirable attributes, but why not go with an obvious choice for the moment—strong arms and chest. Try the total body pushup to get started matching your physical strength to your personality.

1. **Princess Pushup (Assisted).** Let your knees rest on the floor, put your hands on the floor under your shoulders, and push up keeping a straight line from your shoulder to your knees. When you come back down, be sure not to rest on the floor— just keep moving. Do as many as you can. Shoot for 10 to start.

2. Pushup for a Queen (Advanced). If a princess pushup is too easy for you, go ahead and get off your knees and onto your toes. Make sure you keep a straight line from your shoulders to your toes, giving your abs a great workout too.

Princess (Assisted)

Queen (Advanced)

N—Water, Water Everywhere

It sounds easy enough: Drink plenty of water. Once you start paying attention to this, you may be surprised how little nectar of the gods is actually entering your body. Water is nature's medicine and a great energy booster. Track how much water you're drinking. Strive for at least eight 8-ounce glasses a day.

Thoughts from *Day 5*

_____

_____

_____

_____

_____

_____

_____

_____

_____

_____

_____

_____

_____

_____

C—A Better Life

"Jesus told this simple story, but they had no idea what he was talking about. So he tried again. 'I'll be explicit, then. I am the Gate for the sheep. All those others are up to no good—sheep stealers, every one of them. But the sheep didn't listen to them. I am the Gate. Anyone who goes through me will be cared for—will freely go in and out, and find pasture. A thief is only there to steal and kill and destroy. I came so they can have real and eternal life, more and better life than they ever dreamed of'" (John 10:6-10, The Message).

I've come up with some great ideas for a better life. The mundane, challenges, and nuances interrupting my plan usually frustrate me, but what a great relief to know that God wants a better life for me than I can even dream of. Plain and simple: I just have to go through God's gate and he's waiting for me.

R—More Than You Ever Dreamed

What is the one thing you wish for your life? What could make your life easier, happier, and more fulfilling? Jot those thoughts down here:

It may be surprising to realize that as you learn to appreciate your life, those around you, and the One who gave life to you, you already have what makes life full. A full life may be more about perspective than possession.

O—Reflection

Take one of your favorite adornments and give it to a friend. The true beauty of a princess is reflected in those around her. Absorb the moment when your friend shares her thanks for the precious gift. You may feel more beautiful seeing the joy in someone close to you than the mirror could ever share.

W—Lower Body Strength

Although most princesses do get to be paraded around in convertibles during parades, the everyday princess may get to strut her stuff down the street to the grocery store, work, or church on her own two feet. You might as well make them strong. Here's one simple, effective exercise for your lower body that can be done in minutes.

Wall Sit: Stand with your back against a flat wall, move your feet forward about 1.5 to 2 feet, then slide your body down the wall, creating a 90-degree angle at your knees. Hold the position as long as you can. Try for 30 seconds, even if it feels like 30 minutes. Do this three times. Don't forget to stretch when you're done.

N—Veggies

If you're not a veggie person, don't get too worried. There are so many choices out there for you, just keep trying. Start small. When you're craving crunchy chips, try carrots with some light ranch dressing. If you're still craving the chips after a few good vitamins, go for it. If you continue choosing a healthy choice when your cravings are asking for trouble, eventually you can retrain your cravings. Yeah!

Thoughts from Day 6

_____

_____

_____

_____

_____

_____

_____

_____

_____

_____

_____

_____

_____

_____

_____

If the CROWN Fits...

C—Honoring the King

"Let the king be enthralled by your beauty; honor him, for he is your lord" (Psalm 45:11, NIV).

This short passage carries a lot of weight. You must let the King be enthralled with your beauty. (That means no brushing off the compliments or making excuses for what he really means when he says you're beautiful.) And you must honor him with it. (Be beautiful for the Lord— not for the handsome plumber, not so other moms at the PTA are jealous of your new look, but for the *Lord*.)

R—Honor Your Beauty

Beauty is a powerful tool. The pursuit and appreciation of beauty can do great things and can also cause great harm. Denying your beauty can do as much harm as overemphasizing it. Feeling beautiful is not wrong. God wants us to feel beautiful, just as the King is enthralled by your beauty. Recognize your beauty, appreciate your beauty, and honor your beauty. Is the way you present your beauty honoring God? What could you do differently?

O—Plant Seeds of Beauty

What's your favorite flower? Buy some seeds and soil, and plant your flowers. Realize you will have to nourish this potential beauty, just as you have to nourish your own beauty. However, the effort put forth to help both beauties bloom will be well worth it.

W—Appreciate Beauty

Go for a walk. Walk fast enough to get your blood moving a little bit, but the emphasis of today's workout is to appreciate the beauty in your everyday surroundings. Take enough time to really recognize the beauty in your world that God blesses you with day in and day out. Usually people are too busy to notice the squirrel scurrying up the tree or the way the tree branches dance in the wind, playing with the rays of sunshine. Take time to appreciate it today.

N—Eat Something Beautiful

Eat something enjoyable today. Just be sure you appreciate every morsel and thank God for creating those delectable delights.

Thoughts from Day 7

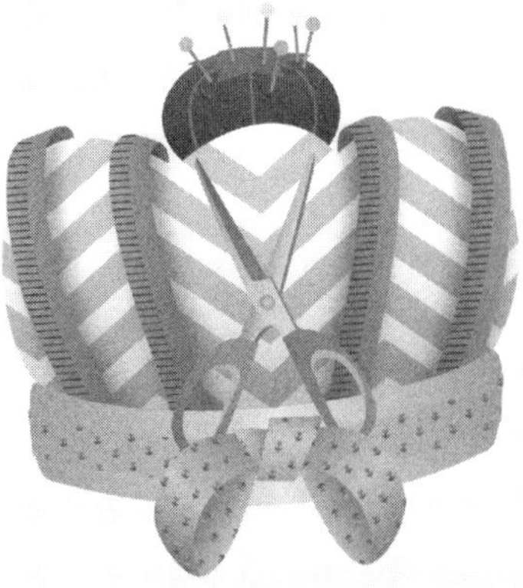

_____

_____

_____

_____

_____

_____

_____

_____

_____

_____

_____

_____

_____

_____

_____

_____

Thoughts from *Day* 7

_____

_____

_____

_____

_____

_____

_____

_____

_____

_____

_____

_____

_____

_____

_____

_____

_____

If the CROWN *Fits...*

C—Set Apart

"I knew you before I formed you in your mother's womb. Before you were born I set you apart and appointed you as my prophet to the nations" (Jeremiah 1:5).

God knew his plans for you before you were born. Maybe you aren't going to be a prophet to the nations, but that doesn't make God's plan for you any less important.

R—Your Purpose

God made you exactly how you are—on purpose. Finding that purpose can be frustrating, exhausting, and painful. However, God is using you every day, and the world would not be complete without you. Just in case you're questioning your path, ask yourself, "How would the world be different without me?" If you're not satisfied with your own answers, ask another question: "What should I be doing differently so I find more meaning in my life?"

O—Display a Masterpiece

Move over, Michelangelo! Here comes a work divinely inspired. *You!* God knew what he had in mind for you before you were conceived. Find an old baby picture of yourself, frame it, and put it in a place for you and others to appreciate daily. Every time you look at those chubby cheeks, remind yourself of how intimately God has been involved in your life regardless of your reciprocation.

W—Child's Pose

A very simple move to stretch out the back. Get on your knees, sitting on your feet. With your arms extended over your head, reach forward to the ground, allowing your chest to touch the ground. Breathe. Enjoy this moment, reflecting on your purpose.

N – Super Food

Time to reach for a super food for a super princess. Super foods contain a tremendous amount of nutrients. One of my favorites is sweet potatoes. Slice them up into sticks (like french fries), spray a pan with nonstick spray, throw on your sweet potato fries, lightly spray the top of the fries with the spray, sprinkle with a dash of salt, and broil for 10 to 15 minutes. Who knew super foods tasted so good?

Thoughts from Day 8

_____

_____

_____

_____

_____

_____

_____

_____

Thoughts from *Day 8*

_____

_____

_____

_____

_____

_____

_____

_____

_____

_____

_____

_____

_____

_____

_____

_____

C—Perfect Love

"Such love has no fear, because perfect love expels all fear. If we are afraid, it is for fear of punishment, and this shows that we have not fully experienced his perfect love" (1 John 4:18).

God offers us a love so great that we have no reason to fear. He's not out to punish us. He already sent Jesus to pay that price for us. God has this amazing, all-encompassing love just waiting for us to reach out for.

R—Send a Letter

Fear holds us back from many things—righting wrongs, reaching out to an old friend, asking for help. Think of someone you haven't been in contact with for more than a year. Sit down, write them a letter, and mail it to them. More than likely your fear is not as big as the love that awaits.

O—New Hair

Change can sometimes be scary. As you embrace your fears, go for a new hair style. What more tangible way is there to announce your freedom from fear than to color or cut or style your precious locks? You don't have to go to some fancy salon; there are many great schools or even at-home color kits. Let loose.

W—Around the Clock

You don't need to be afraid of these crunches. You'll be done in no time. Lay on the floor with your feet resting on the wall (your knees should be at 90 degrees). Bring your belly button to your spine, keep breathing, and start your around-the-clock adventure, lifting your torso slightly off the floor and keeping your neck relaxed:

Crunch directly to the right (3 o'clock) then back to center

Crunch 45 degrees to the right (2 o'clock) then back to center

Crunch straight up (noon) then back to center

Crunch 45 degrees to the left (10 o'clock) then back to center

Crunch directly to the left (9 o'clock) then back to center

Go back around the opposite direction
(9, 10, 12, 2, 3)

Keep going as long as you can. Try for at least three trips around the clock.

Ν—No More Food Fear

Pick a food you've always been curious about but too afraid to try. Tofu, sushi, star fruit, artichokes, soybeans. So many choices. Do a little Internet research if you don't know where to start. Opening your palette to healthy alternatives doesn't have to be scary. Give it a try!

Thoughts from *Day 9*

_____

_____

_____

_____

_____

_____

_____

_____

_____

_____

_____

_____

_____

C—Delight

"Take delight in the Lord, and he will give you your heart's desires" (Psalm 37:4).

Delighting in the Lord is the key point here, not getting all the desires of your heart. Once you start giving God the time he deserves, you will delight in him and perhaps your desires will change too.

R—Bible

The best way to start delighting in the Lord is to spend time with him. One place you know you can find him is the Bible. Yes, that's the book for you. Dedicate 20 minutes to reading the Bible today. If you don't know where to start, Psalms is a great read. Journal a few thoughts on what you read.

O—Girls Night In

You're going to need some extra time delighting in your Lord today, so why not make a night of it? Turn down the lights, have a glass of something sparkly or a latte, and let yourself be enveloped in his love.

W—Strong Arms

The Lord will surely delight in your gun show when you're done with this workout. (Calm down, we all know you're loved whatever the size of your guns, but why not feel strong?) Strong biceps and triceps can be yours. Here are two simple exercises to help make it happen.

- **Basic Bicep Curls:** Grab a weight (a milk jug will work too), keep your elbows in, slowly lower the weight down to your thigh then bring it up to your shoulder, keeping your wrist flat. Repeat. Repeat. Repeat. Shoot for 15 to 20 times.

- **Tricep Dips:** Find a low coffee table or edge of a chair (something sturdy). With your back to the table, place your hands on the table with your fingers gripping the edge. Place your feet as comfortably far away from you as you can, and then lower yourself to the ground, using your arms (not your legs) to create the movement. Rinse and repeat (or just repeat 15 to 20 times).

N—Take a Break From Whippy Beverages

Nutrition isn't only about healthy eating; it's about everything you put in your body, including those yummy mocha frappe extra whip yahdah yahdah yahdahs. Which are oh so yummy and oh so caloric. One of those bad boys can set you back half your caloric allotment for the day pretty quickly. Make a conscious effort to choose water before you go for a sugary drink.

Thoughts from *Day 10*

_____

_____

_____

_____

_____

_____

_____

_____

_____

_____

_____

_____

_____

_____

_____

If the CROWN *Fits...*

$\mathcal{C}$ — No Fear

"I am leaving you with a gift—peace of mind and heart. And the peace I give is a gift the world cannot give. So don't be troubled or afraid" (John 14:27).

Daughters of the King have no reason to fear. God's peace is yours for the taking. Don't get discouraged when it doesn't look the way you expect it to. God's ways are so much bigger than we can understand.

R—What Do You Fear?

Recognizing your fears is the first step in releasing the power they have over you. Fear holds you back from things it has no business keeping you from. What are five things you fear? What are they keeping you from? What can you do to move past that fear?

1.

2.

3.

4.

5.

O—Flourish Not Fear

Buy yourself some flowers. Even if it's just a stem for $1. The natural beauty, life, and peace that accompany this simple gift God has given us is worth it. As you appreciate these flowers throughout the next couple days, ponder how amazing and delicate that plant is and how much more your Creator put into creating you.

W—Lunge Away From Fear

If there is one thing that brings fear into my sphere of influence, it's lunges. These powerful little diddies do so much for your legs and core that you will surely feel what I am talking about tomorrow. Try for 20. Woohoo!

Walking Lunge: With or without weights in your arms, stand with your feet together, step forward with your right foot far enough ahead of you to allow your left knee to come down nearly touching the floor. Remember as you're lunging forward to keep your pelvis tilted under your core and your belly sucked in. It's time to push up with your glutes,  stepping your left foot in front of the right and repeating the process. Once both sides are done, you've completed one repetition. Now only 19 more.

N—Breakfast

After all, mom always said it was the most important meal of the day. Be sure to eat something in the morning so your body has plenty of energy to fight fear all day long. Even just a piece of fruit or a yogurt is a great way to start the day.

Thoughts from *Day 11*

_____

_____

_____

_____

_____

_____

_____

_____

_____

_____

_____

_____

_____

_____

_____

C—Be Blessed

"That is why I tell you not to worry about everyday life—whether you have enough food and drink, or enough clothes to wear. Isn't life more than food, and your body more than clothing?" (Matthew 6:25)

Everyday life often gets in the way of our relationship with God. Although your needs are met, you may feel lacking compared to the Joneses. God urges us to trust our needs will be met and focus on the bigger purpose of life—praising him and sharing God's precious gift of eternal life.

R—Count Your Blessings

It is easy to think your life isn't up to par compared to those around you. However, in a world of credit, *things* aren't necessarily a good indication of someone's blessings in life. Think of five blessings in your life—monetary or otherwise—and thank the One who gave them to you.

1.

2.

3.

4.

5.

O—Inspired Art

Blessings are around you everywhere and your talents are part of those blessings. Take 20 minutes today to create something inspired by the blessings around you. Write a poem, draw a picture, whittle some wood…anything that your heart calls out to capture the essence of your blessings.

W — Breathe

Purposeful breath is much more challenging than it sounds. A lot of today's tasks are introspective, so utilize this time to meditate on your blessings. Sit comfortably on the floor with tall posture and breathe in through your nose, filling your chest and visualizing the oxygen and nutrients filling your entire body down to your fingertips and tippy toes. Relish that moment. Exhale slowly and steadily through your mouth. Repeat this for 5 to 10 minutes. Be sure to get up slowly when you've finished.

N — Fasting

Jesus said specifically that life is more than food. So why not take a day to actively guide your mind to appreciate this life God has given you? Pick a 12-hour time frame to fast, such as 7 a.m. to 7 p.m. Consult a doctor if you have issues with blood sugar or other health limitations.

Thoughts from *Day 12*

_____

_____

_____

_____

_____

_____

_____

_____

_____

_____

_____

_____

_____

_____

_____

_____

C—Trust God's Path

"Trust in the Lord with all your heart; do not depend on your own understanding. Seek his will in all you do, and he will show you which path to take" (Proverbs 3:5-6).

So often we wonder why our plans fail, why things won't go our way. Perhaps we are even looking for God's will, but, all too often, if God's will doesn't match ours, it's hard to accept his path.

R—Trust God

Reflect on the paths that God has presented you. Are you willing to walk them? Spending time reading the Bible gives you opportunity to hear God's voice. If the whispers you are hearing are in line with Scripture, they may just be his will. Are you able to listen to God's gentle calling for you to do something different than what you expect of yourself?

O—Bubble Bath

As you listen for God's whisper, throw some bubbles and bath salts in the bath and dedicate some time to talk to him, the Lover of your soul. This is an amazing opportunity to take your private, relaxed, honest time and share it with the One who cares about you most. Make your heart as soft as your skin.

W — Sun Salutation

This is a basic stretching move that invigorates the entire body. Go through the cycle two times (one for each side of the body) and feel amazing!

N —Water Check

Nature's medicine is calling you. Water helps push all the nasty stuff out of your body, just like trusting God pushes the nastiness of worry and doubt out of your life. Do a little inventory: Are you getting at least 64 ounces of clean, pure water a day? Are you visiting the restroom every 1½ to 2 hours?

Thoughts from Day 13

_____

_____

_____

_____

_____

_____

_____

_____

_____

_____

Thoughts from *Day 13*

_____

_____

_____

_____

_____

_____

_____

_____

_____

_____

_____

_____

_____

_____

DAY 14

C—No Worries (At Least for Today!)

"So don't worry about tomorrow, for tomorrow
will bring its own worries. Today's trouble is
enough for today" (Matthew 6:34).

I love this one. Don't you think it's great that God knows
there is worry and he's not necessarily asking you to
stop worrying...just to focus on today?

R—Clean the Princess Pigsty

Of course it's not a pigsty (you are, after all, a princess),
but the feelings of accomplishment and worth are directly
related to how well you take care of your surroundings. If
your home (or room) is cluttered, chances are so is your
heart and mind. Not only is it a representation of what is
going on in the inside of your princess heart, it is adding
to the chaos of your life. No,
it's not ideal to take 10 minutes
every morning to find your keys
or your shoes or your phone.
Get organized so you have
more time and energy for more
princess-like duties.

O—Pamper the Palace

Now that your kingdom is clean, fill your senses with beauty. Light a couple of scented candles, bake some yummy cookies, or bring in some fresh cut flowers. Something to get your sniffer realizing that beauty exists beyond what is seen. Put on some soft music, cozy up under a comfy blanket, and grab a drink of your choice. Rest in the calmness of clean. Let your mind relax in the comfort of God's graces, closing your eyes and thanking God for all the beauty you don't see every day.

W—Walk the Plank

Although pirates and princesses definitely go together, you're not exactly going to walk the plank. Planks are a pretty straight-forward core exercise. Lay on the floor on your belly. Place your elbows directly under your shoulders; then lift your body up making a straight line from your shoulders to your ankles. Hold the position as long as you can. Try for at least 30 seconds. Relax for a minute then do it again...and again.

$\mathcal{N}$ — Healthy Indulgence

Do a little research (after all, the Internet is amazing) and find a healthy way to make something close to your heart. I like fudge balls made with tons of super foods. Walnuts, dates, cocoa, and vanilla. Healthy definitely can be delicious!

Healthy Fudge Balls

Ingredients:

- 1 cup chopped dates
- 1 cup almonds or walnuts
- 3 tablespoons cocoa
- ½ teaspoon vanilla
- dash of salt

Place almonds or walnuts in food processor and blend until finely ground. Add in dates, cocoa, vanilla, and salt. Blend the ingredients until they are thoroughly mixed and begin to stick together. Roll into small balls and enjoy!

Thoughts from *Day 14*

_____

_____

_____

_____

_____

_____

_____

_____

_____

_____

_____

_____

_____

_____

_____

_____

C—Close Your Mouth

"Watch your tongue and keep your mouth shut, and you will stay out of trouble" (Proverbs 21:23).

How much more to the point can the Bible get? Although there are instances (few and far between for myself) when I regret keeping my mouth shut, I can't even count how many times I've thought I could've said something better or been so much better off just leaving it out. Thanks for the reminder, Lord!

R—Hold Your Tongue

It sounds easy enough, but why is it so hard? As women, we tend to flourish in the gossip of what's going on in the lives of others. There's no way around it, gossip isn't good. If you're saying something that you wouldn't say if that person was around, it probably shouldn't be said. Take some time to think about your motives as you delve into the latest dish of gossip. Are you trying to find solutions for your sister in Christ or are you gaining a little more comfort in how much better your fairy tale is ending? As the Lord's princess, it's your job to look out for his other children. Stop talking about what's happening in someone's life and start asking what you can do.

O—Pretty Princess Polish

If you are ready for today's challenge, go get a manicure or pedicure with a friend (or just invite someone over for a do-it-yourself job). Most of us can attest that salons are the lion's den for an unruly tongue. Pray for God's help to harness your tongue and be an example of his love.

W—Shoulders

Pulling your shoulders back isn't about sticking your chest out. But you don't want to grow up to have a hunched back, so here's a simple exercise to help your posture naturally accept your shoulders in the proper position. (Just remember to think of keeping your shoulders down rather than back—that might help with minimizing the chest advertisement.) With your palms up, hold your arms out from your body (to the sides) and squeeze your shoulder blades together. While in this position make tiny circles with your arms, 20 times in each direction. Feel the burn and the delight of a more confident posture.

N—Grains

Examine your food diary and your diet the past few weeks. Are you making the most of what goes in your mouth? Are you eating refined, white flours? While your royal taste buds may be okay with that, your princess tummy is not as happy. When a grain is refined, most of the fiber is removed, leaving nothing to help clean out your intestines and help grow healthy bacteria. Go for whole grains. Chances are if it's white, it's not right—check the ingredients.

Thoughts from Day 15

_____

_____

_____

_____

_____

_____

_____

_____

Thoughts from *Day 15*

_____

_____

_____

_____

_____

_____

_____

_____

_____

_____

_____

_____

_____

C—Friend

"God–friendship is for God–worshipers; they are the ones he confides in" (Psalm 25:14, The Message).

We all want to be God's friend, but are we putting in the effort that relationship requires? You don't confide in the casual friendships consisting of five minutes over a cup of coffee waiting for church to start. You confide in the close friends whom you've spent countless hours with. Are you God's casual acquaintance or a friend?

R—Focus on Friendship

Invite a friend to lunch, coffee, or on a walk. Pray about whom to invite and for God to guide your conversation. Then pay attention to that friend; really give him or her your full attention. How many times do we take friendships for granted? How often do we take God's friendship for granted? Are we putting in the work required for a good friendship?

O—Friendship Bracelet

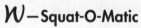

We may not want to relive our junior high years, but we can certainly bring back the great parts. Make, buy, or simply repurpose a bracelet to remind you of your number one friend, Jesus.

W—Squat-O-Matic

A strong relationship needs a strong foundation. Just like your body needs a strong foundation to stand on. Squats are a great way to really feel the burn. Simply stand with your feet shoulder width apart and sit back until your legs are as close to parallel with the ground as you can get. Make sure your knees don't go past your toes so your knees stay healthy. Now squat it out. Do as many as you can. Shoot for 20 squats. Take a break and do it again.

N—Relationship

Take a look at the progress you're making in the realm of nutritional importance. Now put it on the back burner. Making positive choices is, of course, positive. However, if it is consuming your thoughts, your head is not where it should be. A princess needs her King first, not her chocolate (or her lack thereof). Take a few moments to meditate on your relationship with food. Do you put more effort into your meal than your Maker?

Thoughts from Day 16

_____

_____

_____

_____

_____

_____

_____

_____

Thoughts from *Day 16*

_____

_____

_____

_____

_____

_____

_____

_____

_____

_____

_____

_____

_____

_____

_____

C—Quit Comparing

"Make a careful exploration of who you are and the work you have been given, and then sink yourself into that. Don't be impressed with yourself. Don't compare yourself with others. Each of you must take responsibility for doing the creative best you can with your own life."
(Galatians 6:4-5, The Message)

God made you just the way he wanted you. He's given you the challenges and successes you need to do his will. When you start looking at those around you for where you fit on the hierarchy of success, you are only asking for pain.

R—Climbing the Ladder of Comparison

Look at your life and take note of the people you are judging yourself against. What good is this comparative tool anyway? In order to feel better about yourself, someone else must be suffering, and if someone is successful, the comparative ladder of success only points to your demise. Imagine a world where you can feel genuine happiness for another's success and genuine concern for another's troubles. Take yourself out of the compare table and look to those around you with love. You may be amazed at what love comes back your way.

O – The Naked Truth

The moment of truth. No one is around. No control tops, tummy-flattening jean panels, grow-two-cups-in-two-seconds bras. Just you, probably some poor lighting, and a mirror. God made you perfect because you are his. See the beauty in what God has made. It may take more than one time in front of the mirror, but fake it till you make it. Look at this beautiful image and tell yourself, "I like myself the way I am."

W – Climbing the Ladder to Success (Or the Stairs)

Find some stairs and get moving. The more stairs the better, but you can still go up and down if you can only find two stairs. You'll want to take some extra caution if you have any knee issues, but otherwise just move. Think of each step as a trait or possession you tend to apply your comparative scale to. As you step on each stair, think of smashing that need to compare, finding your fulfillment only at the top with the Father in heaven.

After 10 minutes of climbing and obliterating the need to compare, your heart will be pumping, endorphins flowing, and your personal success started.

N – Comparing Sweeteners

Not all sweeteners are created equal. Diet drinks may taste the same as regular drinks, but both have crazy amounts of toxins that your body just doesn't appreciate. Try to eliminate (slowly if you need to) the soda in your life. Try replacing with plain water, lemon water, or water with lemon and stevia for a little sweet tooth. Take note of how you feel with the "real thing" in your body.

Thoughts from Day 17

_____

_____

_____

_____

_____

_____

_____

_____

Thoughts from *Day 17*

_____

_____

_____

_____

_____

_____

_____

_____

_____

_____

_____

_____

_____

_____

_____

_____

_____

C—Created by God

"For through him God created everything in the heavenly realms and on earth. He made the things we can see and the things we can't see—such as thrones, kingdoms, rulers, and authorities in the unseen world. Everything was created through him and for him" (Colossians 1:16).

It's amazing and unfathomable for me to wrap my mind around God creating everything. I know it's true, but trying to comprehend it is a different story for me. It's time to appreciate his creation.

R—Observe Nature

God created everything—the mountains and trees, the dog that won't stop barking across the street, your boss you can't stand, and the lilies of the valley. Get out and enjoy the most basic of God's creations. The earth, the land, the plants...whatever you can find, whether it's a city park or a drive to the country. Enjoy creation.

O—Capturing Creations

Bring a camera on your walk through God's creation. Take photos of the things around you that captivate you and the simplistic, stunning beauty that God has surrounded you with every day. Print out those pictures at home or at a local store and place them around your home or workplace to remind you of the joy that God has for you. He wants to share so much beauty with you every day.

W—Walk, Don't Run

Actually, first you can run. Before you saunter around enjoying God's beauty, walk or run for 15 to 20 minutes to get your heart rate up, and then turn around and walk back on the same path. Notice the difference in the beauty you see when you intentionally open your eyes to God's beauty around you instead of focusing on the task at hand. Try to slow down enough to appreciate all the amazing details God put in your day...just for you.

N—Au Naturel

Enjoying God's simple beauty is the focus of the day, so why not apply it to what you're putting in your body as well? For the entire day eat only "real food." Nothing packaged or processed. Just meat, veggies, fruits, dairy, and some whole grain bread. See how you feel when you fill yourself up with what God has created rather than human imitation.

Thoughts from *Day 18*

_____

_____

_____

_____

_____

_____

_____

_____

_____

Thoughts from *Day 18*

_____

_____

_____

_____

_____

_____

_____

_____

_____

_____

_____

_____

_____

_____

_____

_____

C—New Life

"This means that anyone who belongs to Christ has become a new person. The old life is gone; a new life has begun!" (2 Corinthians 5:17)

I think for many people this verse sounds more like a prison sentence than the joyful freedom it really means. In response to God's love, by giving your life to him you gain a life filled with love and boundaries God shows you to protect you from pain and regret. This new life is a fascinating gift.

R—Inventory *You*

Are you living the life you imagined for yourself? Not necessarily the life of fortune and fame that many of us dream of, but the life that shows who you are as a person. Please do not confuse a Christ-centered life with a boring life. Our God is a God of joy and laughter and fun. But while you are having fun, do you conduct yourself in a way that someone would be surprised to know you are a Christian? What parts of your life might need some adjustment?

O—A New Creation

Just like your new life is being created and expanded daily, you get to create something new in response to the love you feel from God. Take some time to signify this new life and give another gentle reminder of the promise of peace throughout the continuous transition by creating something new and beautiful. Take a picture, paint a painting, write a poem, carve some wood. Make something you can touch or see or even taste that shows the excitement of possibility in a new life.

W—Triangle

You can become a new person one shape at a time. Try the triangle pose and you'll feel strength and stretch through your legs, torso, and arms.

N—New You, New Food

To the direction of living a more uplifted life, give a new food a try. Variety is the spice of life so why not add a little lift to your day with something you've always (or maybe never) wanted to try. Find the brightest, most beautiful piece of produce in the land and enjoy its newfound satisfaction.

Thoughts from Day 19

_____

_____

_____

_____

_____

_____

_____

Thoughts from *Day 19*

_____

_____

_____

_____

_____

_____

_____

_____

_____

_____

_____

_____

_____

_____

_____

_____

DAY
20

C—Cheerful Heart

"For the despondent, every day brings trouble; for the happy heart, life is a continual feast."
(Proverbs 15:15)

The best days are the ones where nothing is different except your attitude. Is your heart happy and cheerful?

R—Serve With a Cheerful Heart

Some days it feels like nothing can go right. Everyone in your life seems to want something, and you seem to get nothing in return. Why do you need something in return? Just for today do something crazy and just do what people ask you—cheerfully. Don't worry about what to expect in return; just give and your heart will be full.

O—Let the Feast Begin

Your heart is cheerful; now it's time to feast, right? Make yourself a candlelit dinner. The meal can be as fancy or as casual as you want; just put some emphasis on the moment. In a world so full of busyness and rushing around, it's rare to enjoy a meal let alone create an event out of it. So turn down the lights, throw on some music, light up the candles, and appreciate a cheerful heart.

W — Belly Laughs

No, seriously, the workout of the day is belly laughs. Look around your world and find something funny in it. If you need some help, call up a friend and rent a funny movie. It seems pretty simple to me. Your choices are to do crunches till your belly hurts or laugh until you feel the same ache. I'm going for a giggle.

N — Enjoy Every Bite

Your feast abounds in front of your eyes, the splendor of the aromas wafting through your nose, and now it's time to dig in. But this is a celebration of cheerfulness and appreciation. You can eat as much as you want in this meal; just make sure every bite makes you happy.

Thoughts from *Day 20*

_____

_____

_____

_____

_____

_____

_____

_____

_____

_____

_____

_____

_____

_____

_____

_____

Thoughts from *Day 20*

_____

_____

_____

_____

_____

_____

_____

_____

_____

_____

_____

_____

_____

_____

_____

C—Giving

"And I have been a constant example of how you can help those in need by working hard. You should remember the words of the Lord Jesus: 'It is more blessed to give than to receive.'" (Acts 20:35)

Hard work usually pays off, especially when you're not necessarily looking for personal gain. It's amazing how much easier, simpler, and happier the world is when giving rather than taking.

R—Step Back

The world continues to push us toward an attitude of individualism that makes "me" the center of the universe and everything that happens in life an attack on who I am. The grouchy woman at the store who had the audacity to ask for your ID when you swiped your credit card, the sister-in-law who never has anything good to say about your brother, or the man who you are certain insinuated that you were fat when he looked at you with "that look." What if for a day we gave not only material possessions but also the benefit of the doubt? What if for a day we tried to step into the shoes of the unbearable person we're encountering? What if for a day we prayed for the people who make us crazy instead of trying to knock them back down the way we feel they do to us?

O—Earrings for Everyone

You know you have a pair of earrings that a friend or not-so-good friend of yours has been eyeing. Share them. Pass on the good of that beautiful little adornment, and see how it makes both your friend and yourself sparkle.

W—Pound Out the Push-Ups

Pushups are a friendly reminder of how hard work can pay off. A simple and convenient exercise that works not only the arms and chest but also the all-important core. It will make carrying groceries to old ladies' cars so much easier. So pound out as many as you can. Shoot for 20, have a rest, and do it again.

N — Share the Nutritional Love

This is not a hall pass to nitpick your closest friends' and family's eating habits. This is a simple opportunity to encourage those you encounter to try something new and healthy. My favorite surprise to pass around to everyone I meet are those delectable fudge balls I mentioned earlier. Yum, yum, yum and so much natural super food. Share it and see someone smile. (Then you can tell them it's good for them.)

Thoughts from Day 21

_____

_____

_____

_____

_____

_____

_____

_____

_____

Thoughts from *Day 21*

_____

_____

_____

_____

_____

_____

_____

_____

_____

_____

_____

_____

_____

_____

C—The Truth

"And you will know the truth, and the truth will set you free" (John 8:32).

Such a simple word—truth. Such a simple concept. Make it happen.

R—Let the Truth Set You Free

Ask God for guidance on today's task. Search your heart and find if there are some truths or half-truths that have been holding you back in a relationship. Often the sadness or anger that travels through our lives with us is the result of guilt, which can be brought on by no one but ourselves. Take the time to let God show you exactly what wrongs you need to right and then...do it. No need to cut calories to feel lighter today.

O—Empty the Closet

Truthfully, how many items in your closet have been hanging there, patiently waiting for their hour of glory, for a year or more? Realize you don't need all the extras "just in case"— you only need Jesus. Shed some weight from your closet, and give them to a family who needs them or donate them to your local mission.

W—Roller Derby

This lower body workout disguised as fun will get your legs burning and your heart smiling. Sit on a rolling chair (like an office chair) with your thighs parallel to the ground. Go as far as you can forward; then go backward. This is so much fun you'll want to do it all day, but you can stop after five minutes if you don't have that kind of time.

N—Caloric Truths

It's time to examine the truth behind what you're eating. You may be surprised how many calories or fat is in some of your favorite snacks. So for only one day, check the labels of everything you're eating and make sure it fits into your plan for healthy living. An average diet is about 2,000 calories. Be sure to compare the serving size to what's on your plate so your estimate is accurate.

Thoughts from Day 22

_____

_____

_____

_____

_____

_____

_____

_____

Thoughts from *Day 22*

_____

_____

_____

_____

_____

_____

_____

_____

_____

_____

_____

_____

_____

C—Beautiful Love

"Promise me, O women of Jerusalem, by the gazelles and wild deer, not to awaken love until the time is right" (Song of Solomon 2:7).

This passage is repeated at least three times in the Song of Solomon. God understands that our hearts and bodies are hardwired for passion. He also understands that this passion can bring him glory—in the right circumstances. A beautiful love is to be appreciated, and like anything worth appreciating, some challenges and sacrifices must be made.

R—Let's Talk About Sex, Baby

Love is such a precious gift that God has given you, and you have the opportunity to accept it as such or to look for a trashy, easier version of it in today's instant gratification society. It is really hard to accept the fact that God's timing and your timing are generally not on the same watch. I'm pretty sure God's timing and my timing aren't even in the same decade. That's because so much of life is instantly mine, and it's so difficult to wait for something that isn't. Are you willing to wait for love? If you already have someone special in your life, is your relationship God-honoring? Are you celebrating the passionate gift God gave your marriage?

O—Projective Messages

What are you projecting? You are a princess, daughter of God. Would someone guess that of you? Assess your appearance, character, and attitude. Are you more like Cinderella's evil stepsisters or gentle, kind Cinderella? One of the most vivid memories of my young adult life is from an evening walk with a couple of friends. I was complaining about wanting to find a good, Christian man. Their response? "Good luck with that. Are *you* even a Christian?" Whoa. My life turned upside down. Of course, it took a few more bad decisions to straighten out my path, but I'm on my way. Are you the person you want to be?

W—Cardio Affirmation

Your body and spirit are so connected that sometimes you can accomplish a lot more when you engage both. Think of the number one attitude or behavior in your life you need to let go of or change. Now consider the positive alternative and run (or walk) until you've convinced yourself of the better option. This activity once took me three miles to even come close, and I had to do it again for a few days but it was worth it.

N—Assess Your Diet

It may be time to check in once more with a food diary. Jot dot everything you're consuming today and compare it to the entries from a few weeks ago. Any changes?

Time	Food	Did I enjoy it?

Thoughts from *Day 23*

_____

_____

_____

_____

_____

_____

_____

_____

_____

_____

_____

_____

_____

_____

_____

_____

C—Actions Speak Louder Than Words

"Dear children, let's not merely say that we love each other; let us show the truth by our actions"
(1 John 3:18).

A wise man once said to judge a man's character by what he does not what he says. Do all you can to let your actions match your words.

R—Love in Action

Love can be as simple as a smile, a hello, or a fresh-baked plate of cookies. Love isn't reserved for boyfriends and husbands, not even for moms and dads, daughters and sons. We are commanded to love the world. Take a moment today to say a kind word to a stranger or someone you don't normally take the time to share a little love with. How does love in action feel?

O—Checklist in Action

Love can be in action in our daily lives. You know that list you have tucked away filled with things you haven't had time to finish? Get it out. Check something off the list. This does

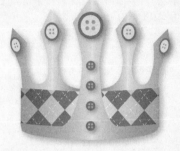

mean you need to actually complete the task before you check it off. This is an opportunity to put the love for yourself and your surroundings in action.

W—Active Stretching

It's time for you to get involved in your stretching, no longer sitting back and passively letting your muscles do all the work. Grab a towel and lay down on the ground. Keep one leg flat on the ground as you lift the other leg into the air, keeping your leg as straight as you can. Wrap the towel behind your calf and assist your leg further into the stretch. Once you've reached the farthest point, hold it there for 10 seconds;

then simultaneously pull the towel toward you and push your leg away from you for five seconds. Then pull both the towel and your leg deeper into the stretch. Repeat this as many times as you'd like, but shoot for at least three times. Now try the other side. Before you know it, you will see a noticeable difference in the flexibility of your hamstrings.

N – Share a Healthy Meal

By now you probably have a few healthy favorites tucked away for your enjoyment. Share it with someone else. Rather than asking why your friend, mom, sister, or husband isn't making better choices, simply invite them over to dinner, bring lunch to work, or even just meet for a tasty snack that may encourage someone else to live a healthier lifestyle.

Thoughts from Day 24

_____

_____

_____

_____

_____

_____

Thoughts from *Day 24*

_____

_____

_____

_____

_____

_____

_____

_____

_____

_____

_____

_____

_____

_____

_____

_____

If the CROWN *Fits...*

C–Right or Wrong?

I have discovered this principle of life—that when I want to do what is right, I inevitably do what is wrong" (Romans 7:21).

Why is it so easy to do what's wrong? Even those with good intentions can easily be drawn to the dark side.

R–Discover Your Angry List

Sometimes we are drawn to what is wrong from all the nasty anger we're hanging on to inside. One way to free yourself from the pain is to find out where the anger is coming from, address it, and let it go. Some things you can control, some things you can't. Figure out which is which and make it happen. Write your angry list out with a marker, hang it on the wall, and as you are able to let go of an anger incident, cross it off the list, never to return to again. Enjoy the freedom.

O—Take Out Your Frustration

Dead skin cells only make you look older and less princess-like. Take out some aggression with a loofah and some elbow grease, showing the radiant glow a princess deserves.

W—Superman Banana

Who is angrier than Superman when he doesn't get his bananas? You…in the middle of this workout, but you'll love it once you're done. Start on your belly and lift your legs and arms up into the air. Then, every five to ten seconds, roll onto your back, lifting your legs and arms off the ground into the shape of a banana. This gets really fun if you have a friend, neighbor, or postal worker help you by shouting out directions. Try to keep this up for a minute. Take a break and do it again.

N – Jedi Mind Tricks

Yes, you want to eat carrots, yet your tummy is telling you cheesy puffs is really what will satisfy you. Or maybe it's the low-fat yogurt full of all that healthy bacteria that is good for you, but your tummy is saying Ben & Jerry's. When you're having a craving today, remember to start with the healthy alternative. Once you've finished a healthy portion, if you're still craving something from the dark side, let yourself have a nibble. Eventually your brain will be tricked into wanting something good.

Thoughts from Day 25

_____

_____

_____

_____

_____

_____

_____

_____

_____

Thoughts from *Day 25*

_____

_____

_____

_____

_____

_____

_____

_____

_____

_____

_____

_____

_____

_____

_____

_____

_____

C—Healthy Fear

"Charm is deceptive, and beauty does not last; but a woman who fears the Lord will be greatly praised." (Proverbs 31:30)

If you've ever looked into the eyes of a truly beautiful 90-and-something-year-old-woman, you'll understand the gravity of this passage. Fear is the utmost form of love and respect. When you realize how big this love is, it can't help but overtake who you are—wrinkles and all.

R—Fear the Lord

When is the last time you really thought about what the Lord of the heavens and earth is capable of? Fear is not simply a matter of being scared of heights, the dark, or your cellphone bill. Fear of God is much bigger than that. This is the Holy of Holies who could not even show his face to those closest to him, even in the Old Testament times, because they would not live through the event. You may think you'd just die if you saw Brad Pitt in person, but that's nothing compared to an encounter with your Maker. Ponder the holiness of God for a moment and what that means to your life.

O—Cross Time

Obviously, there is more to fearing the Lord than making a cross prominent in your life. However, for many it is an excellent reminder of the love that Jesus has given us in the sacrifice he made. It may not sound pretty, but it is also a reminder of what we deserve. God does not owe us a single thing. Rather, quite the opposite. Thankfully, he knows we are incapable of repayment and loves us anyway. Find or create a cross to display in your home or workplace and take a moment to really reflect on what it means to you.

W—Posture Panic

As we come close to the end of our 28 days of growth, it's time to stand a little taller, perhaps literally and figuratively. As you stand tall, imagine a string coming out of the top of your head, pulling your body up and elongating your spine. It might take a little practice to make this the norm for your posture, but a confident princess stands tall for Jesus.

N—Fear the Lord, Not Food

Food issues can control many people, either by eating too much or by severely limiting your intake. If there are moments in your life when you are eating for reasons beyond hunger or not eating despite hunger, hand that emotional distress to the Lord. He can do all things, even help you set down the cookie. Just ask.

Thoughts from Day 26

_____

_____

_____

_____

_____

_____

_____

_____

_____

Thoughts from *Day* 26

_____

_____

_____

_____

_____

_____

_____

_____

_____

_____

_____

_____

_____

_____

_____

If the CROWN *Fits...*

C—Good Advice

"Get all the advice and instruction you can, so you will be wise the rest of your life" (Proverbs 19:20).

As someone who has been cursed with always being right, this passage is a little hard to swallow. It is so simple. Listen and accept. God isn't saying this because you're never right, rather to increase your knowledge in order to gain wisdom.

R—Who Do You Admire?

The Bible often encourages us to involve others in our lives for advice and instruction. Good advice from Christian people who have God's interest first in their minds and then yours. Take a moment to think of someone in your life who you admire. A person who has a pillar of strength you strive for, a friendly smile at always just the right moment, or a helping hand when you have no courage to ask. Now write that person a note expressing your thanks. (Yes, an actual pen and paper note. It will be appreciated.)

O—Out With the Old

Friends definitely aren't accessories; however, who you surround yourself with does make a reflection on you. Take a moment to look at the people in your life who are throwing in their two cents of advice and make sure they are the right kind of influences in your life. If there are people poorly influencing you, it may be time to create some distance in those relationships.

W—Cardio Pal

Call up one of your influential buddies and hit the road, path, cement…whatever! Rather than sitting down for coffee or drinks, be proactive in taking care of yourself physically and emotionally. With all that blood and endorphins flowing you may even think more clearly.

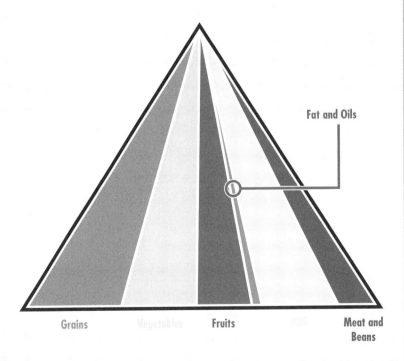

𝒩—Food Guide Pyramid

There are many forms of advice when it comes to nutrition. So many that it is easily overwhelming. The Food Guide Pyramid gives a great example of balanced eating. Try to avoid too much processing and white flours and sugars while including all the yummy goodness from the pyramid, and you'll be a superstar. Find a food pyramid poster you can print and tape inside a cabinet door in your kitchen at choosemyplate.gov/food-groups/downloads/MiniPoster.pdf.

Fat and Oils

Grains Vegetables **Fruits** **Meat and Beans**

Thoughts from *Day* 27

_____

_____

_____

_____

_____

_____

_____

_____

_____

_____

_____

_____

_____

_____

_____

C—Celebration of Joy

"He will take delight in you with gladness. With his love, he will calm all your fears. He will rejoice over you with joyful songs" (Zephaniah 3:17).

The idea of God rejoicing over little ol' me is fascinating. I've done nothing to merit a little "woohoo," let alone an actual shout. Take comfort in knowing your God loves you with such joy he can't hold it in.

R—Celebrate You!

It may not be your birthday, but that is no reason not to celebrate how wonderful you are. God is doing it every day. You have worked hard to become a princess in your eyes and the eyes of others...but God has seen you that way since before you were made. Princesses can definitely be proud of who they are without letting it get out of control, so go ahead and party like it's your birthday!

O—Dress-Up Party

You're celebrating you, so why not invite some friends and have an actual party? Every princess loves an excuse to get dressed up. Call up a friend or two or ten, make some food, turn on some music, and enjoy being the amazing and wonderful princess God intended you to be.

W—Appreciation

You are probably getting in plenty of cardio running around getting ready for your party, so there's no scheduled workout for today. Instead, take some time to appreciate what it feels like to add movement into your life and enjoy the physical capabilities God has given you. Keep it up, Princess!

N—Enjoy!

The very act of eating is a gift God gave you. He could've made us nourished simply from breathing the air around us, but instead he wanted to give us an enjoyable way to sustain our bodies. This gift can be abused either by over or under consumption. If you need more help with one of these issues, there are many great organizations to help you out. Don't be afraid to ask. However, the easiest rule I've come up with is to enjoy every God-given bite you get to take, and when the fun ceases, it may be time to put down the fork.

Thoughts from Day 28

Thoughts from *Day 28*

_____

_____

_____

_____

_____

_____

_____

_____

_____

_____

_____

_____

_____

_____

_____

Additional thoughts

_____

_____

_____

_____

_____

_____

_____

_____

_____

_____

_____

_____

_____

_____

_____

Additional thoughts

_____

_____

_____

_____

_____

_____

_____

_____

_____

_____

_____

_____

_____

_____

Additional thoughts

_____

_____

_____

_____

_____

_____

_____

_____

_____

_____

_____

_____

_____

_____

_____

_____

Additional thoughts

_____

_____

_____

_____

_____

_____

_____

_____

_____

_____

_____

_____

_____

_____

_____

_____

Additional thoughts

Additional thoughts

_____

_____

_____

_____

_____

_____

_____

_____

_____

_____

_____

_____

_____

_____

_____

_____